Terry Pratchett

The Shakespeare Codex

Adapted for the stage by Stephen Briggs

methuen | drama

LONDON · NEW YORK · OXFORD · NEW DELHI · SYDNEY

METHUEN DRAMA
Bloomsbury Publishing Plc
50 Bedford Square, London, WC1B 3DP, UK
1385 Broadway, New York, NY 10018, USA
29 Earlsfort Terrace, Dublin 2, Ireland

BLOOMSBURY, METHUEN DRAMA and the Methuen Drama
logo are trademarks of Bloomsbury Publishing Plc

First published in Great Britain 2021

Cover design: Toby Way
Cover image © Paul Kidby

A catalogue record for this book is available from the British Library.

A catalog record for this book is available from the Library of Congress.

ISBN: PB: 978-1-3502-4497-9
ePDF: 978-1-3502-4498-6
ePub: 978-1-3502-4499-3

Series: Modern Plays

Typeset by Mark Heslington Ltd, Scarborough, North Yorkshire

To find out more about our authors and books visit
www.bloomsbury.com and sign up for our newsletters.

INTRODUCTION

ALL THE DISCWORLD'S A STAGE

The first people *ever* to dramatise the Discworld, in any form, were the Studio Theatre Club in Abingdon, Oxon. That was in 1991, with *Wyrd Sisters*.

We had already staged our own adaptations of other works: Monty Python's *Life of Brian* and *Holy Grail* and Tom Sharpe's *Porterhouse Blue* and *Blott on the Landscape*. We were looking for something new when someone said, 'Try Terry Pratchett – you'll like him'. So I ventured into the previously uncharted territory of the 'Fantasy' section of the local bookstore ('Here Be Dragons'). I read a Terry Pratchett book; I liked it. I read all of them. I wrote to Terry and asked if we could stage *Wyrd Sisters*. He said yes.

Wyrd Sisters sold out. So did *Mort* the year after.

So did *Guards! Guards!*, *Men at Arms*, *Maskerade*, *Jingo*, *Carpe Jugulum*, *The Fifth Elephant*, *The Truth*, *Night Watch*, *Interesting Times*, *Monstrous Regiment* and all the others in the years after that. In fact, 'sold out' is too modest a word for some of the earlier ones. 'Oversold very quickly so that by the time the local newspaper mentioned it was on we'd had to close the booking office' is nearer the mark.

My casts were all happy enough to read whichever book we were staging, and to read others in the canon, too. For the later books in the series, we were often staging the play within a few weeks of the book's publication. I was working from early drafts and the cast was able to read the bound proof.

The books stand on their own, but some knowledge of the wider Discworld ethos is essential when adapting the stories, and can also help directors to find out where it's all coming from, and help the actors with their characterisations.

The Discworld novels have been getting longer, more complex and darker as the years have passed and it is an increasing problem to try to put over the main plot while still meeting the overriding target for amdram – getting into the pub before closing. The important thing is to decide what is the basic plot: anything which doesn't contribute to that is liable to be dropped in order to keep the play flowing. Favourite scenes, even favourite characters, have on occasions had to be dumped. These are hard decisions but the book has to work as a *play*. You can't get 400 pages of novel into two/two-and-a-half hours on stage without sacrifices.

Each play also offers a challenge to Directors in working out who can double for whom in order to stage them with a smaller cast. You'll see from the cast list which follows this Introduction how *we* covered all the roles.

Although the majority of our audiences are 'fans', I've tried to remember when writing the plays that not *all* the audience will be steeped in Discworld lore. Some of them may just be regular theatre-goers who'd never read a fantasy novel in their whole lives – humorous fantasy may not be everyone's 'thing'.

Terry Pratchett: The Shakespeare Codex is based on one of Terry's less well-known stories – the sub-plot which shares the pages of *The Science of Discworld II: the Globe* (plus some bits of other books, such as *Lords and Ladies*). As such, it *may* be better suited to companies with a core of Discworld regulars in their audiences but, then again, the Shakespeare-based plot, and usage of his plots and characters *should* make it accessible to 'normal' theatre-goers. I wouldn't want 'newbies' to feel they were watching something that had been typed on an Enigma machine.

Terry's books are episodic and have a sort of 'cinematic' construction; I have retained this format in *The Shakespeare Codex* and used different stage areas and levels with brisk lighting changes to keep the action flowing. Set changes slow down the action, even when they're really slick. A thirty-second blackout between each scene, accompanied by rustling, crashing and muffled swearing from your stage crew, means you're in danger of losing the audience. Even *ten*-second changes, if repeated often enough, will lead to loss of interest.

I've been to see many productions of the plays and the best have been those that have used bare stages or composite sets – leaving the majority of the 'scene changing' to the lighting technician. The golden rule is: if you *can* do it without scene shifting, *do* it without scene shifting. It's a concept that has served radio drama very well (everyone *knows* that radio has the best scenery). And Shakespeare managed very well without it, too.

The plays do, however, call for some unusual props. Over the years, many of these have been made by my casts and crew: large hourglasses for Death's house, shadow puppets, archaic rifles, dragon-scorched books. Other, more specialised props were put 'out to contract': Death's sword and scythe, an orang-utan, Detritus' head and hands, a Death of Rats, a Greebo, Scraps the dog and two swamp dragons (one an elaborate hand puppet and one with a fireproof compartment in its bottom for a flight scene). Nowadays, I can't imagine how I'd cope without eBay.

Since the Studio Theatre Club started the trend in 1991, Terry and I have had many enquiries about staging the books – from as far afield as Finland, Zimbabwe, Indonesia, Australia, Bermuda and the Czech Republic (as well as Sheffield, Aberdeen, Exeter and the Isle of Man). I even licensed a production of *Wyrd Sisters* in Antarctica! Royalties from the five plays administered by *us* have raised over £90,000 so far for the Orangutan Foundation.

So how did our productions actually go? We enjoyed them. Our audiences seemed to enjoy them (after all, some of them were prepared, year after year, to travel to Abingdon in Oxfordshire from Germany, the Netherlands, Taunton, Edinburgh and . . . well, Oxford). Terry seemed to have enjoyed them, too. He said that many of our members looked as though they had been recruited straight off the streets of Ankh-Morpork. He said that several of them were born to play the 'rude mechanicals' in Vitoller's troupe in *Wyrd Sisters*. He once said that, in his mind's eye, the famous Ankh-Morpork City Watch *are* the players of the Studio Theatre Club.

I'm sure these were meant to be compliments.

THE SHAKESPEARE CODEX

I had wanted to do some sort of adaptation of the Shakespeare plot in *The Science of Discworld II* for some time, but other Pratchett books kept beating that project to the punch. Terry and I had discussed how such a brief plot could work and then, in 2016, the time was finally right. I'm grateful to Rob Wilkins and Rhianna Pratchett for their green light for this one.

We knew from long experience that the Discworld plays were a winner . . . though we'd also learned that the flourishing trade in other groups staging the plays meant that, although they still play to full houses, we couldn't afford to take those full houses for granted.

I wanted to ensure that, even though I had been able to add extra female characters into the mix, that as much as possible of the Discworld characters' dialogue was Terry's own words. I used snippets from *Lords and Ladies*, *Wyrd Sisters* and *Maskerade* to help to flesh out their scenes. I also liked the artifice of using Shakespeare's own words for some of the 'normal' dialogue, and also 'hiding' quotations from his plays in the Discworld scenes.

When I wrote it, I wasn't sure what I was going to call it – *Not the Science of Discworld II*, *All's the Disc's a Globe*, *The Rude Mechanicals*, *A Midsummer Dream's Nightmare*. In the end, I decided to gently pay homage to the *Doctor Who* plot which was very similar to Terry's – the one where the tenth Doctor has to stop Shakespeare completing *Love's Labour's Won* to stop an evil alien invasion – 'The Shakespeare Code'.

A bonus for me was that Abingdon's medieval Unicorn Theatre, with its Globe-esque stage, was a part of the package; it has its shortcomings, but its ambience contributed much to the original success of the shows, and would be a huge bonus in a play set in and around Shakespearean England.

This dramatisation was written with the Unicorn Theatre's restrictions, and the number of players I expected to have available, in mind. Really complicated scenic effects were virtually impossible. Basically, we had a bare stage with an on-stage balcony at the back of the stage with a small curtained area beneath it. Anyone thinking of staging a Discworld play can be as imaginative as they like – call upon the might of Industrial Light & Magic, if it's within their budget. But *The Shakespeare Codex can* be staged with only a relatively modest outlay on special effects. Bigger groups, with teams of experts on hand, can let their imaginations run wild!

In short, though, our experience, and that of other groups, is that it pays to work hard on getting the costumes and lighting right, and to keep the scenery to little more than, perhaps, a few changes of level enhanced by lighting effects and carefully chosen background music. There's room for all sorts of ideas here. The Discworld, as it says in the books, is your mollusc.

Terry Pratchett and me

This was our first Pratchett play since Terry left us, and the first of his shows he wasn't able to come and see – nor to comment on afterwards in the pub, over a large brandy.

I think he would have approved of this riff on that plot, and the opportunity I've taken (with permission from Rob Wilkins and Rhianna Pratchett) to include cameos from a range of Discworld's 'stars' . . . an homage to the character cameos Terry wove into the final Discworld novel, *The Shepherd's Crown*. I've also (as he did in *Dodger*) tinkered a little with the historical timeline to suit the action. Oh, and taken a few *Treehouse of Horror* liberties with some characters' lifelines!

Terry and I became friends and (as you may know) we worked together on lots of projects. It was awful to learn of his 'embuggerance' – posterior cortical atrophy, a form of Alzheimer's – and to know that it would, inevitably, steal him from us. It was a hammer blow when he died.

But Terry's books live on. His plots, characters, humanity and humour are there to delight generations to come.

It's been fun so far, and there are lots of his stories I haven't tackled yet!

Characterisation

Within the constraints of what is known and vital about each character, there is still room for flexibility of interpretation. With the main roles, though, you have to recognise that your audiences will expect them to look as much like the book descriptions as possible. Most drama clubs don't have a vast range from which to choose, though, and it's the acting that's more important than the look of the player when it comes down to it.

Costumes

The City Watch 'style' is English Civil War (though you won't need that for this play), and Angua tends to look slightly 'ancient Roman' with tabbed kilt, etc. Vetinari wears a long, ecclesiastical-looking black robe and a black skull cap. The rest of the city now tends towards Dickensian, with a side order of medieval. The Librarian (for those new to Discworld) is an orangutan. Luckily, orangutan costumes are now more readily available on the internet. For discretion, he also usually wears a robe – we used a red university doctorate robe.

Scenery

Virtually none. We had a couple of stools, and an old-looking table for the inn and for Dr Dee's study. Apart from that, a virtually bare stage, so we could keep the action moving.

Semaphore?

Fans of Terry's books will notice that I've referred to Discworld's 'clacks' system as 'semaphore' in this play. The clacks system is well set up in the novels by its creation in *Going Postal*. Here. it's just a passing reference which would need explaining to audiences unfamiliar with the books. That would just slow down the action and distract from the gags based around the cost of messaging and Granny's one-word reply. If you feel your audiences would prefer 'clacks' to 'semaphore', then feel free to swap.

Oh, and a word on pronunciation . . .

Having seen many of the plays staged, pronunciation of the names seems sometimes to be a stumbling block. Here are some pointers:

Ankh-Morpork	Ankh, as in 'bank', Morpork as in 'more pork', with the stress in the city's name on the second syllable – Ankh-*Mor*pork.
Vetinari	Long 'a' and stress the third syllable – Vetin*ah*-ri.
Rincewind	The 'i's in 'Rincewind' are both short, as in 'dish'.
Angua	Hard 'g'. *An*-Gwa, or *An*-Gewah.
Gytha	Geetha, with a soft 'th'.
Esme	*Ez*-mee. Not Ezmay.
Magrat	As it looks – *Mag*.Rat. stress on the first syllable. Not M'grat, not Margret.

Thinking of staging it . . .?

Application for professional performance, etc., should be made before rehearsal to legal@narrativia.com and for amateur performance to Bloomsbury Publishing Plc at 50 Bedford Square, London, WC1B 3DP, UK (contact@bloomsbury.com). No performance may be given unless a licence has been obtained.

Please also note that we have an obligation to ensure that productions remain true to this approved text. This means that we are now *very* unlikely to agree to text changes unless there are *genuinely compelling* reasons (such as, for example, toning down language for a junior school production).

Stephen Briggs
January 2021
www.stephenbriggs.com
Twitter @StephenPBriggs

Terry Pratchett: The Shakespeare Codex, adapted by Stephen Briggs, was first presented by the Studio Theatre Club at the Unicorn Theatre, Abingdon, on Wednesday 6 April 2016, with the following cast and crew:

On Discworld

Mustrum Ridcully	**Matt Kirk**
Ponder Stibbons	**Brian Mackenwells**
Rincewind	**Dan Booth**
Librarian	**Matthew Fifield**
Havelock, Lord Vetinari	**Stephen Briggs**
Drumknott	**Francesca Richards**
Captain Angua	**Anna Griffiths**
Granny Weatherwax	**Val Shelley**
Nanny Ogg	**Erin Burns**
Magrat Garlick	**Jessica Maguire**
Shawn Ogg	**John Kirchhoff**
Young Esme Weatherwax	**Francesca Richards**
Elf Queen	**Natasha Warner**
Hex	**Suraj Patel**

On Roundworld

Elizabeth I, Queen of England	**Anna Sturrock**
Bess Talbot, Countess of Shrewsbury	**Kat Steiner**
Edward de Vere, Earl of Oxford	**Ben Winters**
William Shakespeare	**Rory Morrison**
Christopher Marlowe	**Charlie Vicary**
Richard Burbage	**Tom Fenton**
Will Kemp	**Mike MacDonald**
Thomas Kent	**Anna Sturrock**
Capulet	**Matt Fifield**
Montague	**Kalil Copley**
Prince	**Charlie Vicary**
Hippolyta	**Kalil Copley**
Dr Dee	**John Kirchhoff**

Lost Hope

Lankin	**Jamie Crowther**
Greysteel	**Simon Wilson**
Vinkala	**Jon Shepherd**
Speck (*non-speaking*)	**Francesca Richards**

On Both Worlds

Narrator	**Mike MacDonald**
Second Narrator	**Jon Shepherd**
Traveller (*cut from this text*)	**Kalil Copley**
Companion (*cut from this text*)	**Jessica Maguire**

Director	Stephen Briggs
Stage Manager	Elena Wright
Lighting	Jon Viner, Nigel Tait
Sound	Daniel Booth

Terry Pratchett

The Shakespeare Codex

An Adventure in Disc and Time

Adapted for the stage by Stephen Briggs

Characters

On Discworld

Mustrum Ridcully, *Archchancellor of Unseen University*
Ponder Stibbons, *a clever wizard*
Rincewind, *an inept wizard*
Librarian, *formerly Dr Horace Worblehat but now an orangutan*
Havelock, *Lord Vetinari, Patrician of Ankh-Morpork*
Drumknott, *Patrician's Secretary*
Captain Angua, *a Watch Officer*
Granny Weatherwax, *a powerful witch*
Nanny Ogg, *a lively witch*
Magrat Garlick, *a herbal witch*
Shawn Ogg, *a Lancre official*
Esme Weatherwax, *a soon-to-be witch*
Elf Queen, *a malicious ruler*
Hex, *a magical thinking device*

On Roundworld

Elizabeth I, Queen of England
Bess Talbot, Countess of Shrewsbury
Edward de Vere, Earl of Oxford
William Shakespeare, *a playwright*
Christopher Marlowe, *a playwright*
Richard Burbage, *an actor-manager*
Will Kemp, *an actor*
Thomas Kent, *a visiting actor*
Capulet, *in Romeo and Juliet*
Montague, *in Romeo and Juliet*
Prince, *in Romeo and Juliet*
Hippolyta, *in A Midsummer Night's Dream*
Dr Dee, *a scientific thinker*

Lost Hope

Lankin, *an elf*
Greysteel, *an elf*
Vinkala, *an elf*

On Both Worlds

Narrator, *a narrator*
Second Narrator, *another narrator*

Act One

Scene One

The Globe Theatre, London. Around 1595. Elizabethan music. As the house lights go down . . . magical lighting effect and sound . . . in the dark the audience hears . . .

Juliet (*off*)   What's here? a cup, closed in my true love's hand?

Poison, I see, hath been his timeless end . . .

First Watchman (*off*)   Lead, boy: which way?

Juliet (*off*)   Yea, noise? then I'll be brief. O happy dagger! (*Noise of dagger unsheathing.*) This is thy sheath; (*noise of stabbing*) there rust, and let me die . . .

Intro music. Lights up. Enter **Prince**, **Capulet** *and* **Montague** *. . . above, a couple of* **Elves** *watch. Throughout the play, the extracts from Shakespeare's plays are played straight. Not hammy.*

Prince   This letter doth make good the friar's words, Their course of love, the tidings of her death:

And here he writes that he did buy a poison of a poor 'pothecary, and therewithal came to this vault to die, and lie with Juliet.

Where be these enemies? Capulet! Montague! See, what a scourge is laid upon your hate,

Capulet   O brother Montague, give me thy hand: This is my daughter's jointure, for no more can I demand.

Montague   But I can give thee more: For I will raise her statue in pure gold; that while Verona by that name is known, there shall no figure at such rate be set as that of true and faithful Juliet.

Capulet   As rich shall Romeo's by his lady's lie; poor sacrifices of our enmity!

Prince   A peace this morning with it brings; The sun, for sorrow, will not show his head:

Go hence, to talk of these sad things; Some shall be pardon'd, and some punishèd;

For never was a story of more woe – than this of Juliet and her Romeo.

Sound of audience applause and cheers. Cast bow. **William Shakespeare** *comes on stage and bows, too. As he walks off, the* **Prince** *says to him:*

Prince   So – Will – we're doing *Richard the Second* next right? – but what's after that? Something a bit lighter, please? A comedy . . .?

William Shakespeare   As it happens, Richard, I *do* have a nice, summery piece in my head . . .

They exit. **Queen Elizabeth I** (*cloaked*) *and two companions enter, carrying programmes for* Romeo and Juliet. **Edward de Vere, Earl of Oxford** *is looking extremely unimpressed.*

Bess, Countess of Shrewsbury (*dabbing her eyes*)   That was so sad . . . I do prefer a laugh, though this tale was very touching, madam . . .

Queen Elizabeth (*still cloaked*)   Oh we also, Bess, we also. Mind you – as you say, this had its moments . . .

She quotes.

'Do you bite your thumb at us, sir?'

Bess, Countess of Shrewsbury (*joining in and acting it out*)   'I do bite my thumb, sir.'

Queen Elizabeth   'Do you bite your thumb at us, sir?'

Bess, Countess of Shrewsbury (*laughing*)   'No, sir, I do not bite my thumb at you, sir, but I bite my thumb, sir.'

They laugh and give a little contented sigh. **Bess** *turns to* **Edward, Earl of Oxford**.

Bess, Countess of Shrewsbury   How many times have we seen it now, Edward?

Edward, Earl of Oxford (*a moment's thought, and with a resigned sigh*)   Eight, Bess. Are we to risk an alehouse this evening . . . 'ladies'?

Queen Elizabeth (*quoting*)   'O, let us hence. I stand on sudden haste.'

They all laugh.

Edward, Earl of Oxford   'Wisely and slow. They stumble that run fast.'

Queen Elizabeth (**Bess** *helps to pull back the hood of her cloak*)   Haha – well you certainly do after a few ales, my Lord of Oxford!

Edward, Earl of Oxford (*bowing*)   Oh, your majesty, that's unjust, I think?

Queen Elizabeth (*laughing*)   We imagine, my lord, it must be painful for you to watch Mr Shakespeare's plays?

She quotes:

'O Romeo, Romeo, wherefore art thou Romeo?

Deny thy father refuse thy name, thou art thyself thou not a Montague, what is Montague? tis nor hand nor foot nor any other part belonging to a man.

What is in a name? That which we call a rose by any other name would smell as sweet . . .'

We think, my lord, you would give a *queen's* ransom to write as well as that . . .?

Edward, Earl of Oxford   Your majesty. I thought you *liked* my plays, ma'am?

Queen Elizabeth   At times, sir, at times. we *did* enjoy 'Zounds! There goes my bodkin!' But, I'sooth, we had partaken of much sack before we viewed it.

She and **Bess** *giggle.*

As you know, my lord, some are *born* great . . .

She gives **Oxford** *a look.*

and some *achieve* greatness . . . (*Nods over shoulder towards theatre.*)

(*To* **Bess**.) Did they say, Bess, what play is next?

Bess, Countess of Shrewsbury   I heard *Richard the Second*, ma'am.

Edward, Earl of Oxford   But he gets murdered!

Bess, Countess of Shrewsbury and Queen Elizabeth   My lord! Spoilers!

They laugh.

Edward, Earl of Oxford (*with a sigh*)   Another tragedy, I mean? God's blood. Why can't they do more like that *Comedy of Errors*? At least *that* was *quite* funny.

He pulls out a manuscript from a bag.

In fact, majesty, I have myself penned a comedy of sorts . . .

Bess, Countess of Shrewsbury (*interrupting him*)   *Comedy of Errors*? *That* was *great*!

(*In a comic servant voice.*) 'I, sir, am Dromio; command him away.'

Queen Elizabeth (*in a comic servant voice*)   'I, sir, am Dromio; pray, let me stay!'

Come on, both of you – first ale's on you, Oxford!

And she runs off, closely followed by **Bess**.

Edward, Earl of Oxford (*following, and adopting a comic old vicar voice*)   'Saint Francis be my speed! How oft tonight have my old feet stumbled at graves!'

(*In his own voice.*) A glove-maker's son? Bloody peasant.

He exits, angrily stuffing away his manuscript.

Blackout.

Scene Two

A hillside in Lancre. The **Narrator** *enters and sits. He/she opens the book they have carried in.*

Narrator   I bet you wondered what had happened to Discworld, yes?

In *Wyrd Sisters*, Granny Esmerelda Weatherwax became the unofficial head of a tiny coven consisting of the easy-going, much-married Nanny Gytha Ogg and young Magrat Garlick, she of the tendency to be soppy about raindrops and roses and whiskers on kittens.

And what took place was a plot not unadjacent to a play about a Scottish king, which ended with Verence II becoming king of the little hilly, forested country of Lancre. He is also now engaged to Magrat.

Let's start at a point about fifty years before the ever-moving now, to a hillside and a young woman, running. Running just fast enough to keep ahead of a young man – although, of course, not so far ahead that he'll give up. Her path takes her to the stone circle known as the Dancers.

It's always quiet around the stones.

A bleak moorland. Mist swirls. Standing stones. Eerie wind, and a noise, of stone grinding on stone. A teenage girl – a younger **Granny Weatherwax** *– walks towards the circle of stones. She stands for a moment.*

Young Esme   I'm here. Show me.

Magical noise/tune. The **Elf Queen** *appears in the circle.*

Young Esme   So you're real, then.

Elf Queen   Of course. What is your name, girl?

Young Esme   Esmerelda.

Elf Queen   And what do you want?

Young Esme   I don't want anything.

Elf Queen   Everyone wants something. Otherwise, why are you here?

Young Esme   I just wanted to find out if you was real.

Elf Queen   And now that you have learned this, what is it that you really want?

Young Esme   Nothing.

Pause.

Why can't you come out from between the stones?

Elf Queen (*ignoring this*)   There must be something that you really want.

Young Esme   You can't come out of the circle, can you? I can go anywhere, but you're stuck in the circle.

Elf Queen   *Can* you go anywhere?

Young Esme   When I am a witch I shall be able to go *anywhere*.

Elf Queen   But you'll never be a witch. They say you won't listen. They say you can't keep your temper. They say you have no discipline.

Young Esme (*snappy*)   Well, they would say that, wouldn't they? But I mean to be a witch whatever they say. You don't have to listen to a lot of daft old ladies who've never had a life. (*Confidently.*) And, circle lady, I shall be the best witch there has ever been.

Elf Queen   With my help, I believe you may. You could be a great witch. You could be anything. Anything you want. Come into the circle. Let me show you.

The girl takes a few steps forward, and then hesitates.

Step through the stones *now*!

The girl hesitates again.

Circle time is nearly over! Think of what you can learn! *Now!*

Young Esme   But –

Elf Queen   *Step through!*

Blackout. The **Narrator** *walks into spotlit area.*

Narrator   But that was a long time ago, in the past . . . that oft-discover'd country from whose bourn no traveller returns.

Narrator *stays on as the scene changes.*

Scene Three

Unseen University, Ankh-Morpork. The **Narrator** *is still on from Scene Two.*

Narrator   So. Once upon a time, there was Discworld. You may have heard of it? Flat world? Carried through space on the back of a giant turtle? And Discworld runs on magic. And the main focus of magical activity on Discworld is at Unseen University.

Well, briefly, Unseen University commissioned a new magical reactor, capable of splitting the *thaum* (the basic particle of magic).

Unfortunately, it produced vastly more magical energy than planned and threatened to explode, destroying the Discworld. The University's thinking engine, Hex, diverted all the magic into creating a space containing nothing – no matter, no energy, no reality and, importantly, no *magic*.

The **Second Narrator** *enters, carrying the Roundworld universe.*

Second Narrator   Phew. Well, unfortunately . . .
the Dean stuck his fingers into that space and 'twiddled'

them, inadvertently creating your little universe. They called *your* world Roundworld, because, in it, matter seems to accrete into balls in space (instead of the far-more-credible discs on the backs of turtles).

Narrator   Time moves differently on Discworld, so they were able to observe your world evolve from an empty planet, through all of your history, through the current time and beyond – right up until your world's destruction . . .

Second Narrator   The Archchancellor appointed Rincewind as the custodian of this new world, which he keeps on a shelf in his room. Here it is . . .

The **Second Narrator** *holds up an illuminated misty ball about the size of a football.*

Your universe. And all would have been well, if only the wizards could stop playing with it . . . They'd messed it around before . . .

Narrator   The wizards created a series of these balls of matter in space, and *accidentally* gave one of them a Moon. This stabilised *your* ball enough that, over a score of millennia . . .

Second Narrator   . . . you remember the wizards can skip over vast periods of your Roundworld time, allowing them to view the entire history of your universe in less than a month . . .

Narrator   . . . *over a score of millennia*, blobs of life emerged, ready to begin evolving into more complex forms.

Second Narrator   There was a crab civilisation and the dinosaurs (both of which are wiped out by comets/asteroids colliding with the earth), before it all jumped ahead to when an advanced civilisation . . .

Narrator   . . . presumably you people . . .

Second Narrator   . . . *an advanced civilisation* . . . evacuated the earth due to an impending natural disaster.

Narrator   Earth explodes, but you people have already wandered off elsewhere. So that all seemed splendid. But they are wizards, after all. As Archchancellor Ridcully himself would have said . . .

Spotlight on **Mistrum Ridcully**.

Ridcully   We're wizards. We're *supposed* to meddle with things we don't understand. If we hung around waitin' till we understood things we'd never get anything done.

Spot out. Lights up at Unseeen University. **Ponder Stibbons** *is on stage, with a portable* **Hex** *device and a small bottle with a note in it.* **Rincewind** *enters. The* **Narrator** *gives the ball to* **Rincewind**, *who puts it into his bag.*

Stibbons (*holding out the bottle*)   Rincewind! Read this – it's from the Archchancellor – he's on Roundworld again.

Rincewind (*reading*)   'Get here at once. Am in Roundworld. Bring Librarian. Food good. Beer awful. Wizards useless. Elves here too. Dirty deeds afoot. Ridcully.'

Narrator (*as he/she leaves*)   It isn't that Archchancellor Ridcully is stupid. Truly stupid wizards have the life expectancy of a glass hammer. He has quite a powerful intellect, but it is powerful like a locomotive, and runs on rails and is therefore almost impossible to steer.

Stibbons   Elves?

He takes out his portable **Hex** *device.*

Stibbons   Hex – why?

Hex (*a voice, off, over the speakers*)   Elves have entered Roundworld. It is to be expected. Their world is a parasite universe. They need a host.

Stibbons   Do you understand this?

Rincewind   No, but I've run into elves. Well, run *away* from them actually. You don't hang around elves. But why are they there? There's nothing *on* Roundworld at the moment!

Stibbons   But I thought you'd done a paper on the various species that keep turning up and then dying?

Rincewind   You read that?

Stibbons   You said every so often some intelligent life turns up, hangs around for a few million years, and then dies out because the air freezes or the continents explode or a giant rock smacks into the sea . . .

Rincewind   That's right. Last time I looked, it was a ball of ice again.

Stibbons   So what's the Archchancellor doing down there?

Rincewind   Drinking beer apparently.

Stibbons   When the whole world is frozen?

Rincewind   Maybe lager . . .?

Stibbons   But he, and the senior faculty, are supposed to be running around in the woods, pulling together, solving problems and so on.

Rincewind   On Roundworld?

Stibbons   No – in woods about fifty miles away! Not in a glass globe in your study . . . (**Rincewind** *opens his bag.*) in your bag . . .?

Rincewind   How did the bottle get out?

Hex   I did that. I maintain a watch on Roundworld.

Stibbons   So why didn't you tell us the Archchancellor needed help?

Hex   He was having such fun trying to send the bottle.

Rincewind   So can't you just bring *them* out, too?

Hex   Them?

Stibbons   The Archchancellor and faculty.

Rincewind   So. Can you bring them back?

Hex   Yes.

Stibbons   In that case –

Rincewind   Hold on! Can you bring them back *alive*?

Hex (*affronted*)   Certainly. With a probability of 94.37 per cent.

Stibbons   Not bad odds, but 5.63 per cent is still quite a big margin of error. Perhaps –

Rincewind   Quite! Humans aren't bottles. How about alive, with a fully functioning brain and all organs and limbs in the right place . . .?

Hex   There will be unavoidable minor changes . . . I cannot guarantee reacquiring more than one of every organ . . .

Pause.

Is this a problem?

Rincewind   Maybe there's another way?

Stibbons   What makes you think that?

Rincewind   The note asks for the Librarian.

Stibbons   Good spot!

He starts to exit.

Rincewind (*as he exits*)   And then I really think we ought to see the Patrician!

Stibbons (*as the lights black out*)   Oh gods!

Blackout.

Scene Four

The heath, Lancre. **Nanny Ogg**, **Granny Weatherwax** *and* **Magrat Garlick** *storm on separately, and simultaneously.*

Granny Weatherwax   In the middle of my bloody herb garden!

Magrat   In Verence's broad beans!

Nanny Ogg (*carrying a saucer of mustard and cress*)   Poor little mite! And he was holding it up to show me, too!

The other two give her a look.

Our Pewsey was growing mustard-and-cress on a flannel for his nan. He shows it to me, and just as I bends down – splat! Crop circle!

Granny Weatherwax   This is serious. It's been years since they've been as bad as this. We all know what it means, don't we.

Magrat   Um . . .?

Granny Weatherwax   What we've got to do now is –

Magrat   Excuse me.

Granny Weatherwax   Yes?

Magrat   *I* don't know what it means. I mean, old Goodie Whemper –

All three put a finger to the side of their nose and bob once as they say . . .

All Three   – maysherestinpeace –

Magrat   – told me once that the crop circles were dangerous, but she never said anything about why.

The older witches share a glance.

Granny Weatherwax   All you need to know for now is that we've got to put a stop to 'Them'.

Magrat   What 'Them'?

Granny Weatherwax (*radiating innocence*)   The . . . circles, of course.

Magrat   That's not what you meant! You said 'Them' as though it was some sort of curse. It wasn't just a them, it was a *them* with a capital The.

The old witches look awkward again.

Nanny Ogg   No harm in telling her about the Dancers, at any rate.

Granny Weatherwax   Yes, but . . . you know . . . I mean . . . she's Magrat.

Magrat   What's that meant to mean?

Nanny Ogg   We're talking about the –

Granny Weatherwax   Don't name 'em! They'll come if you names them!

Nanny Ogg   Yeah, right. Sorry. But, no reason any of these circles will open *in* the Dancers . . . We can always hope . . .

Granny Weatherwax   But if one *did* open up inside the stone circle . . .

They exchange knowing looks.

Magrat   You just do this on purpose! You talk in code the whole time! You always do this! But you won't be able to when I'm queen!

Nanny Ogg   Oh? Young Verence popped the question, then?

Magrat   Yes!

Granny Weatherwax   When's the 'happy event'?

Magrat   Two weeks' time. Midsummer Day.

Nanny Ogg   Bad choice. Shortest night o' the year –

Granny Weatherwax   Gytha Ogg!

Nanny Ogg   Queen Magrat, eh? Cor.

Magrat   Well, anyway, I don't have to bother with this sort of thing. Whatever it is. It's your business. I just shan't have time, I'm sure.

Granny Weatherwax   I'm sure you can please yourself, your going-to-be-majesty.

Magrat   Hah! I can! You can jolly – you can *damn* well find another witch for Lancre! All right? Another soppy girl to do all the dreary work, make the tea and never be told anything and be talked over the head of the whole time. I've got better things to do!

Granny Weatherwax   Better things than being a witch?

Magrat   Yes!

Nanny Ogg (*quietly*)   Oh, dear.

Granny Weatherwax   Oh. Well, then I expect you'll be wanting to be off. Back to your palace, I'll be bound.

Magrat   Yes!

She stalks off.

Nanny Ogg   You daft old besom, Esme.

Granny Weatherwax   You know what she'd say if we told her. She'd get it all wrong. The Gentry. The Lords and Ladies. Circles. She'd say it was . . . nice. 'Glamorous'. Best for her if she's out of it.

Nanny Ogg   They ain't been active for years and years. But even though they seems to be leaking magic into the kingdom, I still can't sense them *here*. Not actually here – in Lancre.

Granny Weatherwax   No . . . they're close, and *not* close. Not Lancre. On the Disc, and not actually on the Disc, I think.

Nanny Ogg   Wha . . .?

Granny Weatherwax   We need to go to Ankh-Morpork.
Someone's been meddlin'.

Nanny Ogg   Unseen University?

Granny Weatherwax   Of course. Wizards.

Blackout.

Scene Five

An inn in Elizabethan England. On stage are **Will Kemp** *and a couple of other actors.* **Shakespeare** *enters with* **Richard Burbage**. *When, as here, the characters are speaking lines taken from Shakespeare, it's important that they speak those lines as naturally as possible.*

William Shakespeare   Is all our company here?

Will Kemp   You were best to call them generally, man by man.

Richard Burbage   Here is the scroll of every man's name.

Will Kemp   First, good Master Burbage, say what the play treats on, then read the names of the actors, and so grow to a point.

Richard Burbage   Marry, our play is *The Life and Death of King Richard the Second*.

William Shakespeare   A very good piece of work,
I assure you.

Richard Burbage   Answer as I call you. Will Kemp . . .

Will Kemp   Ready. Name what part I am for, and proceed.

Richard Burbage   You, Master Kemp, are set down John of Gaunt, Duke of Lancaster.

Will Kemp   What is John of Gaunt? A lover, or a tyrant?

William Shakespeare   A noble man, who mourns for lost England under Richard's reign.

Will Kemp   That will ask some tears in the true performing of it: if I do it, let the audience look to their eyes; I will move storms . . .

William Shakespeare   You get a great speech. Read us a little, Master Kemp. That top page will do – your main speech . . .

Will Kemp (*reading* (*delivering this speech 'properly'*))
     'This royal throne of kings, this scepter'd isle,
     This earth of majesty, this seat of Mars,
     This other Eden, demi-paradise,
     This fortress built by Nature for herself
     Against infection and the hand of war,
     This happy breed of men, this little world,
     This precious stone set in the silver sea,
     Which serves it in the office of a wall,
     Or as a moat defensive to a house,
     Against the envy of less happier lands,
     This blessed plot, this earth, this realm, this England,
     This –' . . . do I get any jokes?

William Shakespeare   No, Will Kemp, this is a *tragedy*!

We hear the creaking timbers of a Tudor building under strain from magical power. This announces the elves' presence.

Richard Burbage   But, masters, here are your parts: and I am to entreat you, request you and desire you to con them by tomorrow night and meet me in the King's Head, a mile without the town, by moonlight; there will we rehearse. For (as you know) if we meet in the city, we shall be dogged with company, and our devices known. In the meantime I will draw a bill of properties, such as our play wants. I pray you, fail me not. The play's the thing, gentlemen.

Will Kemp   Well, if it were done 'twere well it were done quickly. We will meet; and there we may rehearse most courageously. Take pains; be perfect: adieu.

Richard Burbage   At the King's Head we meet.

Shakespeare *and the others exit . . . The* **Elves** *creep in after them and watch them walk off . . . the creaking timbers die away . . .*

Elf Queen   So – a new world. A round world. Not dull and flat, like Discworld. And this time, there will be no defeat. The *land* will welcome us. It must hate humans too. There is no magic at all on this world. People believe in magic, but it doesn't work here. They will *believe* anything, though. I mean – did you see that *Romeo and Juliet*? Suggestible, pliant minds.

Lankin   But there are witches.

Elf Queen   Yes, but poor things, *poor* things. They're not like Discworld witches. They're just old women. I have crept about, my deary. I have crept about o'nights. I know the *wizards* they have here, too. They are just street magicians, conjurers, tricksters . . . powerless.

Lankin   I remember the witches on Discworld.

The **Elves** *hiss.*

Lankin   Minds like . . . like metal. Like . . . iron.

The **Elves** *shudder at the thought of this metal.*

Elf Queen   The time is right, Lankin. Their minds. They won't be able to resist the pull of our power. And they do not know about the power iron has over us.

We have waited centuries for this world to develop a species worth playing with; worth torturing and killing.

Now that this Roundworld has simple-minded *humans* for us to control, we can return in force.

Lankin   And then we can torment them. (*The other* **Elves** *laugh in malicious glee.*) When? *When?*

Elf Queen   Soon. *Soon.*

Exeunt.

Scene Six

Patrician's Palace, Ankh-Morpork. **Granny Weatherwax** *and* **Nanny Ogg** *are on stage.*

Nanny Ogg   Remind me. What are we doin' here, Esme? At the Patrician's Palace? I thought we was going to the University?

Granny Weatherwax   We were in Ankh-Morpork for twenty minutes, Gytha. Twenty minutes.

Nanny Ogg   Sorry, Esme.

Granny Weatherwax   I can't have witches being done down, Gytha. You've been exploited. Swindled out of your life savings.

Nanny Ogg   Two dollars?

Granny Weatherwax   Well, it's all you'd actually *saved*.

Nanny Ogg   Only 'cos I spent everything else. Some people salt away money for their old age; I prefer to accumulate memories.

Granny Weatherwax   Well, there you are, then.

Nanny Ogg   I *was* putting those two dollars by towards some new piping for my still up at Copperhead. You know how that scumble eats away at the metal –

Granny Weatherwax   You were putting a little something by for some security and peace of mind in your old age.

Nanny Ogg   You don't get peace of mind with my scumble! Pieces, yes; but not peace.

It's made from the finest apples, you know. Well, mainly apples.

So – why are we here?

Granny Weatherwax   Because, Gytha, you were conned out of your life savings and that Commander Vimes is apparently out playing with his son while crime runs rife in his city.

Nanny Ogg   I'm not sure that's actually what they . . .

Granny Weatherwax (*ploughing on*)   I *assumed* that two harmless old ladies would've been safe in a city like Ankh-Morpork.

Lord Vetinari is clearly losin' his touch. The City Watch Commander is on a swan. So we have to see his boss. *Then* we'll talk to Mr Ridcully!

Drumknott *enters.*

Drumknott   Ah, er, ladies . . . sorry to have kept you waiting. King Verence did send us a message that you might be visiting our city. If you would come this way? I'll show you into His Lordship's ante room.

Nanny Ogg (*as they exit*)   Ante room? We ain't his aunties! . . .

They exit as the lights blackout.

Scene Seven

The Patrician's Palace, Ankh-Morpork. **Drumknott** *ushers in* **Rincewind**, **Stibbons** *and the* **Librarian**. *A moment, and then* **Lord Vetinari** *enters.*

Lord Vetinari   Good morning, gentlemen. I understand from Drumknott that you have an emergency . . .?

Drumknott   My lord! I apologise – the matter is, it seems . . .

Rincewind   . . . *extremely* urgent! Er, my lord . . .

Lord Vetinari   Ah. Rincewind. You little scamp.

Stibbons   My lord, it seems that the Archchancellor is in trouble on Roundworld . . .

He hands **Vetinari** *the message bottle.*

Lord Vetinari (*reading it*)   I *thought* we had agreed not to interfere there again?

Stibbons   Yes, my lord. But . . .

Vetinari *waves him to continue.*

As you know, sir, all times on Roundworld are accessible to us . . .

Lord Vetinari   . . . Yes, yes, in the same way that all pages of a book, though consecutive, are accessible to us.

Stibbons   Indeed. And I have ascertained that the Archchancellor, the Senior Wrangler, the Chair of Indefinite Studies and Senior Tutor are on Roundworld. But not at the 'present time' – they are many years in Roundworld's past! I don't know how they got there – but Hex has located them. They sent a message out in a bottle, but they don't seem to be able to get back themselves . . .

Rincewind   . . . At least not in one piece . . .

Lord Vetinari   Wizards mean libraries. You have brought the Librarian . . . This is going to be about L-space, isn't it? They say they have found elves on this Roundworld? And other wizards . . .?

Rincewind   He does say they're useless . . . my lord.

Librarian   Oook.

Lord Vetinari   . . . so that means libraries. That implies you can get through using L-space . . . which joins all libraries in the multiverse, yes?

Rincewind   Well, yes, but . . .

Granny *and* **Nanny** *breeze in.*

Granny Weatherwax   Blessings be upon this house.

Elves? You've let elves infest your Roundworld, Mr *wizard*?

Drumknott   Excuse me, ladies, how did you get in here?

Granny *holds up a hand.* **Drumknott** *stops.*

Granny Weatherwax   Through the door, young man.
(*She gives him a hard look.*) But I expect you have other things
to do?

Drumknott   No. I'm fully occupied here with my . . .

Granny Weatherwax (*a little more firmly*)   Which I am sure
you can deal with better – *in another place.*

Drumknott *exits.*

Granny Weatherwax (*to* **Nanny**)   I'm losing my touch, that's
what it is. Getting old, Gytha.

Nanny Ogg   You're as old as you feel, that's what I
always say.

Granny Weatherwax   That's what I mean. The Lords and
Ladies are planning to control this . . . Roundworld thing.
They will torture, torment and kill. We should . . . help.

Nanny Ogg   Ain't you scared?

Granny Weatherwax   No. But I hope they is. I'm too
prideful, that's what I am. But I don't hold with paddlin'
with the occult. Once you start paddlin' with the occult you
start believing in spirits, and when you start believing in
spirits you start believing in demons, and then before you
know where you are you're believing in elves. And then
you're in *trouble*.

Rincewind   But all those things exist!

Granny Weatherwax   But that's no call to go around believing in them. It only encourages 'em.

Nanny Ogg   Oooh, it's true what they say. You're a prideful one, Esmerelda Weatherwax.

Granny Weatherwax   Who says that?

Nanny Ogg   Well, you did. Just now. I'm not saying you couldn't beat them – we done it once before, didn't we?

Granny Weatherwax   We can't leave fightin' elves to wizards! We have to stop them.

Nanny Ogg   Must we?

Granny Weatherwax   Can't stop myself, that's my trouble.

Nanny *is silent.*

Granny Weatherwax   And I loses my temper over the least little –

Nanny Ogg   Yes, but –

Granny Weatherwax   *I hadn't finished talkin'!*

Nanny Ogg   Sorry, Esme.

Lord Vetinari   We're talking about elves, yes? I thought all that was just folklore.

Granny Weatherwax   Of course it's folklore, you stupid man!

Lord Vetinari   I do happen to be Patrician, you know.

Granny Weatherwax   You stupid Patrician, my lord.

Lord Vetinari   Thank you.

Granny Weatherwax   Folklore doesn't mean it's not true! Maybe it gets a little muddled over the years. Folks forget *why* they do things. Like the horseshoe thing. It's nothing to do with the shape. It's coz it's a handy bit of iron to hang over the door – elves can't go through a door that's guarded by iron!

Elves are cruel for fun. They can't understand that anything else might have feelings. They project this . . . glamour.

When people look at them, they see beauty, they see something they want to please.

But when elves get into a world, *everyone* is slaves. They take what they want, and they want everything.

Nanny Ogg   There's an old Lancre saying, Mr Patrician – 'Elves are wonderful. They provoke wonder. Elves are terrific. They beget terror.'

Lord Vetinari   Very picturesque.

Stibbons   Their power derives from the use of a mental ability that one might describe as 'glamour' to confuse and over-awe people, my lord. Socially, elves rather resemble bees. They have a Queen and a King, whose attitude towards one another is chilly contempt for most of the time. They also resemble bees in being very sensitive to weak magnetic fields, which gives them their absolute sense of position and direction. Elves always know exactly where they are.

Rincewind   It's also the cause of their traditional hatred of iron, because this distorts the local magnetic field and leaves them panicky and powerless.

Lord Vetinari (*to* **Granny Weatherwax**)   I think your help would be welcome, Mistress Weatherwax.

(*To* **Rincewind**.) But why can't Ridcully and the others come back by themselves? Surely they used magic to send back the bottle?

Granny Weatherwax   Maybe you should just go and ask them?

Librarian   Oook!

Rincewind   He says L-space is only to be used to travel outside the University by very senior wizards. It's not some kind of magic funfair ride.

Stibbons   But this is an order from the Archchancellor! It's the only way we can get there!

Lord Vetinari   It seems to me there *is* a way of travelling in L-space without actually travelling at all. If you put the globe inside the UU Library . . . then that would mean that, even though you are, in theory, travelling in L-space, you wouldn't *actually* be moving anywhere outside the Library . . .

He looks at the **Librarian***, who shrugs resignedly.*

Rincewind   That's true, my lord – the globe would be inside the Library, (*to* **Stibbons**) so even if you travelled to Roundworld, you'd only have really travelled a few feet. The globe is only infinite on the *inside*, after all!

Stibbons   If we put the globe on the Librarian's desk, the whole journey would take place inside the Library? The Library is safe, Rincewind – so no harm will come to us.

Rincewind   What do you mean, 'us'?

Stibbons   We'll find them and bring them back.

Rincewind   There's elves there!

Lord Vetinari   That has to be verified.

Rincewind   They are dangerous!

Lord Vetinari   Oh, Rincewind, do you not know that cowards die many times before their deaths? The valiant never taste of death but once. Hm?

Rincewind *gives* **Lord Vetinari** *a look of total lack of understanding.*

Granny Weatherwax   What I don't get is why the elves are on this Roundworld. What's there for them to be interested in?

Rincewind   Last time I checked they hadn't even discovered the *potato*. The *potato*! I mean – can you *imagine*?

Lord Vetinari   Setting aside, momentarily, your well-known predeliction for cooked tubers . . . can we revert to the subject of elves?

Rincewind   They like to have slaves . . . there's nothing there that's bright enough to be a slave.

Stibbons   Not quite true. Hex says that *currently* Roundworld is in what it refers to as the sixteenth century; maybe things have changed, again.

Lord Vetinari   I think that Mrs Ogg and Mistress Weatherwax may be best employed back in Lancre to guard the stone circle there, in case the elves attempt to return to *this* world. King Verence's semaphore message says there are crop circles . . . which would seem to imply a possible weakness near the stone circles. They must be guarded, too.

Granny Weatherwax   That's right, your lord. There's been things going on. All the bracken and weeds was trampled around the stones. I reckon someone'd been *dancing*.

Nanny Ogg (*genuinely shocked*)   Dancing? Up here? You never told me that!

Granny Weatherwax   There's still power in those stones. Not much, but the ring is holding.

Nanny Ogg   But who'd be daft enough to go up there and dance around the stones? Lucky we left Magrat to keep an eye on 'em.

Granny Weatherwax   Hmpf. Her trouble is she's too flighty. Soppy. She thinks you can lead your life as if fairy stories work and folk songs are really true.

Nanny Ogg   Hope she does all right as queen.

Granny Weatherwax   We taught her everything she knows.

Nanny Ogg   Yeah. D'you think . . . maybe . . .?

Granny Weatherwax   What?

Nanny Ogg   D'you think maybe we ought to have taught her everything *we* know?

Granny Weatherwax (*to* **Nanny**, *after a moment*)   Would've taken too long.

(*To* **Vetinari**.) You're right, your lord. Gytha and I do need to be in Lancre.

(*To* **Stibbons**.) You wizards can wiz off to your Roundworld.

Lord Vetinari (*to* **Ponder**)   I must insist, though, that you are accompanied by a senior officer of the City Watch, as my representative, as it were. I will send a message for Captain Angua. She will be able to help you detect the presence of elves.

Stibbons   And of course you – Rincewind. You are the only other person who knows anything about Roundworld. You *have* to come with me.

Librarian   Oook.

Stibbons   With *us*.

Lord Vetinari   Yes, Rincewind. Run along and sort it out. Let me know how it goes.

Blackout.

Scene Eight

A room in Elizabethan London. On stage is a small table, set with a pewter inkwell and quills, a tankard and a few ancient books.
Rincewind, **Stibbons**, *the* **Librarian** *and* **Captain Angua** *enter. There is a muted creaking of timber.*

Rincewind   Hello?

The **Librarian** *crosses to a desk and picks up a book. He hands it to* **Rincewind***.*

Rincewind   Alchemy? Oh dear. That stuff doesn't even work on *our* world.

Stibbons (*using a thaumometer*)   Oh dear. I'm reading a very high glamour quotient.

Angua   So there actually *are* elves here?

Stibbons   It's practically *elvish*, according to Hex. The Archchancellor was right. Hex, can you still communicate with us?

Hex   Certainly. You will need to tell people that the Librarian is Spanish.

Stibbons   What's Spanish?

Librarian   Ook.

Hex   It's a country about five hundred miles from here.

Angua   And their people look like the Librarian?

Hex   No. But people here would be quite prepared to believe so. This is a credulous age. The elves have done a lot of damage. The humans' greatest minds spend their time studying magic, astrology, alchemy and communion with spirits.

Rincewind   Well? Sounds like life at home.

Hex   Yes. But there is no narrativium here. No magic. None of those things work.

Angua   Then why don't they give up?

Hex   They believe it *should* work – if only they get it right. Someone is approaching . . .

Rincewind   Run away!

Ridcully *enters. He seems unsurprised to see them.*

Ridcully   Ah good. Y'made it then? Who's the Spaniard?

Angua   It's the Librarian, Archchancellor.

Ridcully   Oh yes. Sorry. Been here too long.

Stibbons   We came as soon as we could, sir. How long has it been, for *you* here?

Ridcully   Couple of weeks. Funny how soon you get to all their religious conflicts – and the heads on spikes at the city gates . . . so unlike our dear old Ankh-Morpork. (*He indicates the thaumometer.*) You've detected elves?

Dr Dee *enters and potters over to the desk. At this point, he is totally unaware of the Discworld group.*

Hex   It is all right. I have, for the moment, arranged things so that he can neither see nor hear us.

Stibbons (*speaking sotto nonetheless*)   The place is lousy with glamour, sir.

Ridcully (*thumbing over his shoulder at* **Dr Dee**, *and speaking quite loudly*)   Chap who lives here spends all his spare time trying to do magic.

Angua   We might be invisible, Archchancellor, but we're *not* deaf!

Stibbons   Trying to do magic which doesn't work here.

Ridcully   Right. But everyone believes it does. That's what elves do to a place. It seems that the Lost Kingdom of the Elves has gateways into Roundworld as well as Discworld. They have stone circles here, too . . .

Stibbons   . . . so *that's* why some of their glamour leaked out into Lancre . . .

Ridcully (*crossing to* **Dr Dee**)   Told this chap I'd dropped in from another sphere. Seemed to work. But it's a mad world. No narrativium. People makin' up history as they go along.

Brilliant men spendin' their time tryin' to work out how many angels can dance on the head of a pin.

Dr Dee *collects a book and exits.*

Stibbons   Sixteen.

Ridcully   Yes. *We* know that because we can go and look. *Here* it's just another silly question. It's a mess.

Angua   Well, *you* made it!

Rincewind (*to* **Angua**)   We didn't make it *this* badly!

(*To* **Ridcully**.) Any sign of potatoes, sir?

Ridcully *shakes his head.* **Rincewind** *sighs.*

Angua   But anyway – do we have the right to interfere? Lord Vetinari briefed me on your previous adventures. You didn't before – all those other civilisations you encountered in previous visits here! . . .

Stibbons *and* **Ridcully** *gasp – the* **Librarian** *says Ook'.*

Angua   Sorry – but you didn't. I gather they all got completely wiped out by ice ages and falling rocks and you never did anything to stop it. I mean, elves are just another problem, right? And we know the species is either intelligent enough to survive them or it ends up buried in the bedrock like all the others.

Ridcully   But with no narrativium, it doesn't know how the story is meant to go. So of course we have to interfere. We're wizards. And *we* know where they're going.

Stibbons   Yes – in a thousand years or so it's going to be hit by a really big rock.

Angua   But I thought you found there'd been a race that built huge structures to get off the place.

Stibbons   That's right, Captain.

Angua   *Can* a new species emerge in only a thousand years or so?

Stibbons   I don't think so.

Ridcully   You mean *these* are the ones that leave?

Stibbons *and* **Rincewind** *nod.*

Ridcully   I think we're going to be here for some time.

We hear the creaking timbers that announce elvish activity.

Stibbons (*to* **Ridcully**)   By the way, sir – where are the others? The Senior Wrangler? The . . .?

Ridcully (*clearing his throat*)   Ah, yes. Yes, well, good question . . . erm –

Magical effect. The **Elf Queen** *enters, with some others. One carries a small cage, containing small wizard figures.*

Elf Queen   Welcome to my world, gentlemen – oh, and 'lady'.

Ridcully   *Our* world!

Elf Queen   Let us continue to disagree, shall we? *You* may have constructed it, but it's *our* world now!

Ridcully   We have iron, you know.

Elf Queen   Much good may it do you, here. It didn't help your little friends –

The **Elves** *hold up the cages . . . the* **Elf Queen** *moves over and speaks to the caged people.*

Elf Queen   Aw . . . So cute. Little Discworld wizards. But so very, *very* fragile. Such a shame about the Senior Tutor.

She produces the Senior Tutor's miniature body and hands it to an **Elf**, *who bites off its head and eats it. She turns back to* **Ridcully**.

Elf Queen   You intend to fight *here*? When you have no magic? Be serious. You should be grateful; this is a world without narrativium. Your strange humans are monkeys without stories. They don't know how the world is supposed to go. We gave them stories and made them people. And now they are worth controlling. Worth playing with. Worth tormenting.

Ridcully   You gave them gods and monsters. Stuff that stops people thinkin' straight. Superstitions, demons, unicorns, bogeymen.

Elf Queen   You have bogeymen on your Discworld.

Angua   Yes. We do. But they're not in our minds – they're on the *outside*, where we can see them and deal with them. When you can *see* them, they don't have any real power.

Rincewind   Like unicorns. When you *meet* one, it's just a big sweaty horse. Looks nice, smells sweaty.

Elf Queen   And it's *magical*!

Ridcully   Yes, but that's just another thing about it. Big, sweaty, magical. Nothing '*mysterious*'. You just learn the rules. Sorted.

Elf Queen   But you should be *pleased*! Everyone here thinks this world is just like yours! Many people even believe that it's flat!

Stibbons   Yes, but back home they'd be *right*. Here, they're just ignorant!

Elf Queen   Well, there is not a thing any of you can do about it. This is our world. It's all belief. The religions here – amazing! The crop is bountiful and the harvest is rewarding. Do you know that more people believe in magic on this world than on your own?

Angua   We don't have to *believe* in magic! It *works*!

Elf Queen   Well, they *believe* in it here – and it *doesn't* work! And thus they believe in it even more, while ceasing to believe in themselves. Isn't it astonishing?

Here you – even you so-called wizards – are nothing. But *we* understand this world and we have time to cultivate it. We *like* it. You can't take us away. We are part of their world now . . . They are here for our amusement . . .

Stibbons This world, madam, has about another thousand years before all life is wiped out.

Elf Queen (*lightly*) Ah well. There are other worlds.

Ridcully That's all you have to say?

Elf Queen What else *is* there? Worlds begin and end. That is how the universe works. That is the great circle of existence.

Ridcully The great circle of existence, madam, can eat my underwear.

Elf Queen Fine words. You are good at concealing your true thoughts from me, but I can see them in your face. You think you can still fight us and win. You have forgotten that there is *no* narrativium here. It does not know how stories should go. Here, the third son of a king is probably just a useless weak prince. An old lady gathering wood in the forest and muttering 'lawks' is probably just an old lady and not – as on your world – almost certainly a witch.

Oh, there is a *belief* in witches. But here, a witch is merely a method of ridding society of burdonesome old ladies and an inexpensive way of keeping a fire going all night. Here good does not automatically triumph in the end. Here, evil is generally defeated by a more organised kind of evil. *My* world. Not yours. Good day to you.

Magical effect. She disappears. The creaking timbers fade.

Ridcully Quite well spoken, for an elf. Good turn of phrase.

Angua What did they have in those cages, sir? Was that . . .?

Ridcully   Yes, Captain. That was my senior faculty – the Senior Wrangler, Indefinite Studies . . . (*looking off*) . . . Senior Tutor. The elves captured them.

Stibbons (*looking off, then back at* **Ridcully**)   They killed the Senior Tutor. As flies to wanton boys, are we to the elves. They kill us for their sport.

(*No reaction from* **Ridcully**.) Sir? They *killed* the Senior Tutor!

Ridcully   Yes, well. Spooky bugger.

Angua   And that's it? We can't do anything?

Stibbons   We don't have any magic.

Ridcully   But we know everything is goin' to turn out all right, right? We know these people get off this planet just before the next big wallop, right?

Stibbons (*with a sigh*)   Well, yes and no, sir. The elves have now changed the 'story', as it were. Hex thinks the elves did something to the monke[ys] . . . er, something to the prima[tes] . . . to the *somethings* that evolved into . . . humans.

Stibbons *does not complete the words 'monkeys' or 'primates' as he is aware they may be offensive to the* **Librarian**.

Ridcully   Interfered with them?

Stibbons   Yes, sir. We know they can affect people's minds when they sing . . .

Ridcully   And you're goin' to say it's because of 'quantum' at some point?

Stibbons   I hadn't planned to, but you are on the right lines.

Angua   You said – 'became humans'?

Stibbons   Yes. It's how things happen here. Things become other things. At least, *some* of some things become other things. It's not how things work on *Discworld*, but Hex says that is how things work *here*. Hex calls it 'evolution'. Can we accept for a moment, sir, that this is true?

Ridcully   For the sake of argument?

Stibbons   Well, for the sake of not *having* an argument, sir.

Ridcully   All right then.

Stibbons   And we know, sir, that elves can really affect the minds of lesser creatures . . . They must have loved humanity once they found it. Humanity was very creative, when it came to being frightened. They were good at filling their future full of dread.

Ridcully   Which gives the elves control?

Stibbons   Yes. But they can still spoil everything by using that wonderful, fear-generating mind of theirs for thinking up things to take the fear away – like calendars, locks, candles – and stories. Stories are where the monsters die.

Ridcully   So. Any thoughts?

Rincewind   We could go to the pub?

Ridcully   No. This is serious.

Rincewind   So was I.

Angua   I don't see what we can do. You think the elves have manipulated the humans' past to make sure they'd be compliant, yes?

Librarian   Oook.

Rincewind (*to the* **Librarian**)   But Ponder wants us to all go back and stop the elves. Ambush them before they can do anything. I don't think that will work.

Librarian   Oook?

Rincewind   Because it's Plan A. And Plan A is guaranteed to fail. Narrative fact.

Ridcully I know someone who'd be right at home with this problem. Mister Stibbons, could we get home now, to send a semaphore message?

Stibbons Yes, but we don't need to. Hex can do that directly.

Ridcully How?

Stibbons I, er, connected him up to the semaphore just after you left, sir . . .

Ridcully So Hex can send and receive messages?

Stibbons Erm . . . yes, sir, but . . .

Ridcully But that costs a *fortune*! I hope it's coming out of your budget, because . . .

Stibbons Er, no, sir . . . because it's actually quite cheap. Er, it's free, actually. Hex has deciphered the access codes for the city's Guilds, sir, and it just adds the odd message to their transmissions . . . they never really notice . . . so . . .

Ridcully So . . . we're *stealing*?

Stibbons Well, yes, sir, in a way, but . . .

Ridcully This is very disturbing news, Stibbons.

Stibbons Yes, sir.

Ridcully I feel I must ask you a rather difficult and worrying question. Is it likely that anyone will find out?

Stibbons Oh, no, sir – it's impossible to trace.

Ridcully Oh, well that's all right then.

Stibbons (*relieved*) You wanted a message sent, sir?

Ridcully Yes. To the Kingdom of Lancre. They've only got the one semaphore tower. Ready?

Ponder *takes out the portable* **Hex***.*

Ridcully 'To Mistress Esmerelda Weatherwax . . .'

As **Ridcully** *speaks, we hear his recorded voice continuing the message which then segues into the Interval music.*

How are you? I am fine. An interesting problem has arisen, and I'd be grateful for your input. This is a message from Mustrum Ridcully. As you know, we are on Roundworld, inside the universe which currently sits on a desk in the Library of Unseen University . . .

Interval.

Act Two

Scene One

Granny Weatherwax *is on. We hear* **Ridcully**'s *message again, fading in from the Interval music.* **Shawn Ogg** *enters and starts to read the message out loud. As he does, the recorded* **Ridcully** *version fades out.*

Shawn Ogg (*walking across the stage*)   'To Mistress Esmerelda Weatherwax . . . How are you? I am fine. An interesting problem has arisen, and I'd be grateful for your input. This is a message from Mustrum Ridcully. As you know, we are on Roundworld, inside the universe which currently sits on a desk in the Library of Unseen University . . .'

By this time he should have reached the 'door' and knocked.

Granny Weatherwax (*she picks up a large pine cone and makes as if to throw it*)   I warn you – I'm fed up with you lads always on the ear'ole for three wishes . . .!

Shawn Ogg   It's me, Mistress Weatherwax! I wish you'd stop doing this!

Granny Weatherwax   See? You ain't havin' another two!

Shawn Ogg   No, no – I've just come to deliver this for you . . . it's a semaphore message from Ankh-Morpork for you, Mistress Weatherwax! It's only the third one we've ever had!

Granny Weatherwax (*taking the paper from him*)   What's one o' them things?

Shawn Ogg   It's like a letter that's taken to bits and sent through the air.

Granny Weatherwax   By them towers I keeps flyin' into?

Shawn Ogg   That's right, Mistress Weatherwax.

Granny Weatherwax (*short pause as she starts to read it*)   They moves 'em around at night, you know.

Shawn Ogg   Er . . . I don't think they do . . .

Granny Weatherwax (*bridling*)   Oh? So I don't know how to fly a broomstick right, do I?

Shawn Ogg (*quickly*)   Actually, yes, I've remembered . . . They move them around all the time . . . On carts. Big carts. They . . .

Granny Weatherwax   Yes yes. Be quiet now.

She reads.

'To Mistress Esmerelda Weatherwax. How are you? I am fine. An interesting problem has arisen, and I'd be grateful for your input . . .'

She skim-reads through the fairly long message.

Ha! Silly old fools think they can't see the wood for the trees, and the trees *are* the wood!

She skim-reads a little more.

Hmpf. Cost a lot, does it, sendin' messages like this?

Shawn Ogg   That message cost more than 600 dollars! I counted the words! Wizards must be made of money!

Granny Weatherwax   Well, I ain't. How much is one word?

Shawn Ogg   Five pence for the sending and five pence for the first word.

Granny Weatherwax   Ah. I've never been one for numbers, but I reckon that comes to . . . sixpence and one half penny.

Shawn Ogg (*with almost no pause*)   That's . . . right.

Granny Weatherwax   You have a pencil?

Shawn *hands it over. She writes one word and hands him the paper.*

Shawn Ogg   That's all?

Granny Weatherwax   Long question, short answer.

She turns away from him. **Shawn** *holds out a hand for the money.*

Granny Weatherwax   Was there anything else?

Shawn Ogg (*realising he had better not push the money thing – or ask for his pencil back*)   Er . . . No.

He exits.

Granny Weatherwax (*holding up her newly acquired pencil*) Right then.

Blackout.

Scene Two

A room in Elizabethan London. **Stibbons**, **Ridcully**, **Angua** *and* **Rincewind** *are on.*

Stibbons   Plan A seems to be working fairly well. We've gone back in Roundworld's time and adjusted their past to help humans to develop in a way that will put them in the right state to deal with the elves . . . despite *their* attempts to block us. We do seem to have, er, *assisted* the elves in the evolution of what I might venture to call Homo Narrans – 'storytelling man'.

Rincewind   Still no potatoes, I notice . . .

Angua (*ignoring him, to* **Stibbons**)   There's still religious wars. And still the heads on spikes. Do you think the elves have encouraged that . . .?

Stibbons   Yes, I think possibly so. That's humans for you, Captain. Imagination gets used for everything. Wonderful art, and really dreadful instruments of torture.

Rincewind   Heads on spikes. No potatoes, but heads on spikes.

Stibbons   Do stop going on about that, Rincewind. It was only two heads.

(*To* **Angua**.) What was that country where the Archchancellor got food poisoning?

Angua   Italy, I think. The rest of us had the pasta.

Stibbons   Well, it's full of churches and wars and horrors and some of the most amazing art . . .

Angua   Most of which they'd copied from that book you'd showed them a few hundred years earlier!

Stibbons   Yes, well – we have to get them ready to escape this planet in a few million years – they can't be left to do it all themselves.

Rincewind   I still think we said too much to that artist with the bald head. The one who looked like Leonard of Quirm? You shouldn't have told him about Leonard's flying machine.

Stibbons   He scribbled a lot of stuff . . . it won't matter. Anyway, who'll remember an artist who can't even get a smile right.

Rincewind   And what about that man who was painting that chapel ceiling for that man in the white robe in . . .

Angua   Rome? Mr Buonarotti and the Pope? I think it will look a lot better with those pictures painted on it. Much more interesting than the plain coat of distemper the Pope had asked for . . .

However, Archchancellor, I *don't* think it was wise to tell that balding civil servant all about the Discworld. That young man with the cats and the insectivorous plants. You may have changed what he could grow up to be.

Ridcully   Nonsense. 'To be' or *not* 'to be' . . . that's the trousers of time – ha! He was much too busy with his unclear power station.

Angua   Nuclear. But he was making notes . . .

Stibbons (*aside to* **Angua**)   It'll be fine. That special recipe I gave him for banana daiquiri will make him forget everything.

Ridcully (*looks around*)   The place looks normal, after all. Trees grow, clouds stay up in the sky . . .?

Stibbons   If you remember sir, this universe has things which work instead of narrativium, sir.

Rincewind   Remember those big lizards? They lasted for millions of years. They were quite successful, surely?

Ridcully   Successful? Did they build a single university?

Rincewind   Well, no . . .

Ridcully   Did they draw a single picture? Invent writing?

Rincewind   Not that I know–

Ridcully   And they all got killed off yet another big rock hittin' this world.

They all sigh.

Hex   A message has arrived.

Ridcully   From Lancre? That was quick.

Hex   Yes. The message is unsigned. It is: THEOSTRY.

Stibbons   'THEOSTRY'?

He looks at the screen.

T-H-E-O-S-T-R-Y

Ridcully   What does that mean? Rincewind – this sort of thing is right up your street, right?

Rincewind   The semaphore people charge by the word, don't they?

Ridcully   Yes. It's scandalous! Five pence a word, on the long-distance trunk . . .

Rincewind   And this was sent by an old woman in Lancre, where as far as I recall the chicken is the basic unit of currency? Not much money for fancy messages, then.

Looks to me like a simple anagram of – THE STORY.

Angua   I think it means – 'change the story', at a saving of ten pence.

Ridcully   But we've tried changing it.

Angua   Change it in a different way, perhaps? At a different time? We have L-space. Can't we get advice from any books written in different futures?

Librarian   Oook.

Stibbons (*to the* **Librarian**)   I'm sorry, sir, perhaps the library rules don't apply here . . .

Ridcully   Look at this way, old chap . . . the rules do apply, of course, but if we get this wrong then any libraries that *do* still exist here in a thousand years' time will be destroyed in a fireball and/or entombed in ice . . .

Librarian   Oook, oook.

Ridcully   I'm glad you see the point. But the elves are still here. All we've done so far is do their work even better – I don't see how we can stop them!

Angua   So – belief doesn't have the same power on this world as it does on ours, right? But it's still pretty strong. And even so, the elves *are* here and they're pretty strong.

Rincewind   But we know they feed on people. They play with them like cats play with mice or injured birds. They'd happily pull a person apart just to see what happens. Like the Senior Tutor.

Ridcully   Yes, yes. They're not nice.

Stibbons   They are such stuff as nightmares are made on.

Rincewind   We want them to go away, and I have a plan.

Ridcully   You have a plan? You?

Rincewind   These people may have progressed a lot, but they need to do better if the'yre to become the people who escape this world before its destruction. Well, I want us to move this world into the path of history that contains someone called William Shakespeare. The man who wrote this.

He pulls out a piece of paper. **Ridcully** *takes it.*

Ridcully (*reading* (*straight*))   'What a piece of work is a man! How noble in reason, how infinite in faculty! In form and moving how express and admirable! In action how like an angel, in apprehension how like a god! The beauty of the world. The paragon of animals . . .'

And this man lives *here*?

Rincewind   Potentially.

Ridcully   This man stood knee deep in muck in a city with heads on spikes and wrote *this*?

Rincewind   Yes! In this world – potentially – he is the most influential playwright in the history of the species! Despite needing a lot of tactful editing by most directors, because he had his bad days just like the rest of us!

Ridcully   By 'this world' you mean –

Stibbons   Alternative worlds. In one of the many alternative histories.

Angua   You mean he should be here but he isn't?

Rincewind   The leading playwright in *this* city is Arthur J. Nightingale.

Angua   Is he any good?

Rincewind   He is the best they have. Objectively, he is dreadful. His play *King Rufus III* is widely considered the worst play ever written.

Angua   So Shakespeare's not here, then?

Rincewind   Not yet. But, if we arrange things correctly, he will write this – the Librarian got me copies through L-space . . .

He hands around modern published editions of A Midsummer Night's Dream.

This is another play he will write, has written, has been about to write . . . I think it could be very important in . . . helping this world to deal with the glamour of the elves . . .

Ridcully (*flipping through it*)   Some of this looks a bit familiar. A lot of this really happened.

Rincewind   Yes. And I think that's because he'll write it after talking to *you*. We need him. This is a man who can tell the audience – *tell* them – that they are watching a bunch of actors on a stage and then make them *see* a huge battle, right there, in front of their eyes.

Ridcully   Huge battle? Did I miss that?

Stibbons   Different play, sir.

Ridcully   So we have to make sure this man exists here and writes this play in this world? Why?

Stibbons   Ah – that's Plan B. Rincewind?

Rincewind   Well, it's all about seeing is believing. We don't believe in chairs. Chairs are just things that *exist*.

Ridcully   So?

Rincewind   We don't believe in things we can see. We believe in things we *can't* see.

Ridcully   And?

Rincewind   And I've been checking this world against L-space and I *think* we've made it the one where the humans survive. Because now they have gods and monsters. And when you can *picture* them, you don't need to *believe* in them any more.

Ridcully   Nevertheless, we have no magical powers here, so we still need to be careful. We've done the best we can. Your plan, Rincewind?

Rincewind   We need to ensure our book-reading and playgoing humans see elves and fairies as merely amusing fictional creations.

So they need to believe that they *don't* exist.

First, we have to make this world the kind this William Shakespeare can turn up in. Some travelling may be involved. Back in time . . . for thousands of years. But first, let's see if we have done enough already. Hex – is this world ready for the William Shakespeare of whom we spoke?

Hex   It is.

Rincewind   And he exists?

Hex   No. Two of his grandparents did not meet. His mother was never born.

Ridcully   Right. I think we've learned from our previous experiences. This is at least a simple problem. We shall need a length of string, a leather ball of some kind and a large bunch of flowers . . .

They all exit – sound effect – lighting effect – then they re-enter, one carrying some flowers.

Rincewind   Hex – is this world ready for the William Shakespeare of whom we spoke?

Hex   It is.

Rincewind   And he exists?

Hex   Violet Shakespeare exists. She married Josiah Slink at the age of sixteen. No plays have been written, but there have been eight children of which five have survived. Her time is fully occupied.

They all exchange glances.

Angua   Perhaps if we offer to babysit?

Ridcully   Too many problems. Still, it's a change to have an *easy* one for a change. We'll need the probable date of conception, a stepladder and a gallon of black paint.

They all exit – sound effect – lighting effect – then they re-enter, one carrying a can of paint.

Rincewind   Hex – is this world ready for the William Shakespeare of whom we spoke?

Hex   It is.

Rincewind   And he exists?

Hex   No. He was born, successfully survived several childhood illnesses but was shot dead one night while poaching game at the age of thirteen.

Ridcully   We're getting there – and another easy one. We shall need, let me see . . . some drab clothing, a dark lantern and a very large cosh.

They all exit – sound effect – lighting effect – music – they re-enter and re-exit several times, each times appearing with one of them carrying a bizarre item. Finally they re-enter, one carrying a police helmet.

Rincewind   Hex – is this world ready for the William Shakespeare of whom we spoke?

Hex   It is.

Rincewind   And he exists?

Hex   Yes.

Angua   Alive? Male? Sane? Not in the Americas? Not struck by a meteorite? Not killed in a duel?

Hex   No. At the moment, he is in the tavern that you frequent.

Ridcully   Does he have all his arms and legs?

Hex   Yes. And – Arthur J. Nightingale was never born. And the potato has been discovered.

Rincewind   Hot damn. Chips!

Blackout.

Scene Three

The Globe, London. On stage are **Shakespeare**, **Kemp**, **Burbage**, **Kent** *and others. Creaking timbers. As the scene starts,* **Lankin** *and other* **Elves** *enter and lurk. They remain invisible to the actors. As the scene progresses, they prod and tease at the humans, stealing script pages . . . pinching them . . . eating their food, etc.*

Will Kemp   Are we all met?

Richard Burbage   Yes, yes . . . and here's a marvellous convenient place for our rehearsal.

Will Kemp   Master Shakespeare . . .

William Shakespeare   What sayest thou, Will Kemp?

Will Kemp   Write me a prologue; and let the prologue say we will do no harm with our swords, and that Richard is not killed indeed; and this will put the audience out of fear.

Richard Burbage   We have no need of such a prologue, Will Kemp. Come, sit down, every mother's son, and rehearse your parts. It's Act One, Scene Two – John of Gaunt and the Duchess. And both – speak the speech, I pray you, as *I* pronounced it to *you*, trippingly on the tongue. Thomas Kent – you begin with the Duchess's speech at line 65 . . .

Thomas Kent (Duchess)   Where then, alas, may I complain myself?

Will Kemp (John of Gaunt) *(gesturing wildly)*   To God, the widows' champion and defence.

William Shakespeare   No, no – do not saw the air too much with your hand. Like Thomas, suit the action to the word, the word to the action. We aim here to hold the mirror up to nature. Thomas . . .?

Kent *speaks the* **Duchess**'s *speech as* **Lankin** *and* **Vinculus** *speak over it.*

Lankin (*speaking over the* **Duchess**'s *speech below*)   What hempen home-spuns have we swaggering here . . . (*laughing*)

Vinculus (*speaking over the* **Duchess**'s *speech below*)   A play? So near the cradle of the Elf Queen? Let us watch . . . there may be mischief to be had.

Thomas Kent (Duchess)   Why, then, I will. Farewell, old Gaunt. // Thou goest to Coventry, there to behold

Our cousin Hereford and fell Mowbray fight: // O, sit my husband's wrongs on Hereford's spear,

That it may enter butcher Mowbray's breast! // Farewell, old Gaunt: thy sometimes brother's wife // With her companion grief must end her life.

Will Kemp   Must I speak now?

Richard Burbage   Ay, marry, must you.

Will Kemp   I'faith, Burbage, this play is not very humorous.

Richard Burbage   It is a *tragedy*, Will Kemp.

Will Kemp   So was *Romeo and Juliet*. (*To* **Shakespeare**.) Come on, Will – can we not do the other one first? That weaver role might have been written for me!

Thomas Kent   That, Will Kemp, is because it *is* being written for you.

Richard Burbage   The people *do* like a comedy. And money, it's true, is a little tight.

Thomas Kent (*to* **Kemp**)   I'm sure they'll pay to see your Bottom!

The actors all laugh.

William Shakespeare   That, I trow, is a gag that might oft be repeated in future years, Master Kent. But the midsummer play is not yet finished. It gives me problems in the writing . . . it needs . . . *something* . . .

Will Kemp   In that case, let's to the Boar's Head. Ale will help us all to work out the plotting

General agreement. They start to exit. One of the group (an expendable one) starts to collect sheets of manuscript from the floor.

Richard Burbage (*as they depart, his arm around* **Shakespeare**'s *shoulder*)   Does it have a dog?

William Shakespeare   Yes, yes, Richard, there's a part for Toby. I was in two minds at first – I thought Toby, or not Toby? But then I thought – the mechanicals stage a play for the nobles, you see, and of course Moonshine traditionally . . .

Richard Burbage   . . . has a dog?

William Shakespeare   He does.

Richard Burbage   Excellent.

Shakespeare *goes.* **Burbage** *speaks as he follows.*

Richard Burbage   And what about *pirates*?

The **Elves** *watch. The expendable actor has finished picking up the scripts. They stand for a moment. An* **Elf** *walks to him, touches him on the heart for a second. He drops dead. The* **Elves** *giggle as they exit. Blackout.*

Scene Four

A street in London. The heroes are on their way to the Boar's Head.

Stibbons   Hex is sure it's this way, Archchancellor.

Hex   At the next corner, turn left. Midden Lane. Then, you have reached your destination.

Creaking timbers . . . lighting effect. The **Elf Queen** *appears, with supporters.*

Elf Queen   What are you doing?

Ridcully   Er . . . just a little – what are we callin' it, Stibbons?

Stibbons   A sociological experiment, sir.

Fairy Queen   You've been teaching them art! And sculpture!

Angua   And music. Mister Stibbons is rather good with a lute, it seems.

Stibbons   Only in a very amateur way, I'm afraid.

Ridcully   Dashed easy t'make, a lute – tortoise shell and some sinews and you're away. I meself have been re-aquaintin' meself with the penny whistle – though Rincewind's expertise with the comb and paper leaves somethin' t'be desired . . .

Angua   Any chance of having the Senior Wrangler back? He's an expert on the orpharion?

Elf Queen   And *why* are you doing all this?

Ridcully   You're not angry, are you? We thought you'd be pleased. We thought you *wanted* them this way. You know . . . imaginative.

Elf Queen   You are *planning* something! Why should you help us? You told me to consume my underthings!

Ridcully   Well, it's not as though their world is *worth* fightin' over. Well – pub calls. Day to yer!

They breeze past her – blackout.

Scene Five

The Boar's Head, London. **Shakespeare** *is alone at a table, with a tankard of ale. He has a manuscript and is looking at it sorrowfully. A flamboyant, romantic-looking man enters (***Christopher Marlowe***). He is carrying two tankards and crosses to* **Shakespeare***.*

Christopher Marlowe (*plonking one tankard in front of* **Shakespeare**)   Will, how goes it? May I?

Shakespeare *gestures for him to join him.*

Christopher Marlowe   I hear great things of your 'Romeo and . . . erm –'

William Shakespeare   Juliet.

Christopher Marlowe   Of course, sorry – I have not seen you since draft . . . seventeen. I am sorry not to have yet made it to a performance, but I have been busy myself. (*Glumly.*) *The Massacre of Paris.*

William Shakespeare   A comedy?

(*Sighs heavily.*) Not going well?

Christopher Marlowe (*taking a drink*)   No it does not . . . What are you working on?

William Shakespeare (*showing him the battered manuscript*) *Richard the Second.*

Christopher Marlowe   What happened to the fairy play?

William Shakespeare   I couldn't make it work. I cannot properly engage the lovers, the fairies and the inevitable rude mechanicals.

Christopher Marlowe   Will, Will, please tell me you have changed the weaver's name?

Shakespeare *shakes his head with a wry smile.*

Christopher Marlowe   Seriously? But the *Queen* may attend your play!

William Shakespeare   The Queen *has* a bottom, Kit.

Christopher Marlowe (*laughing*)   That may be so, Will, but it wouldn't do to talk that way in public!

Have you thought, Will, of having your weaver become besotted with the Fairy Queen . . .?

William Shakespeare   But how . . .?

Christopher Marlowe   She and the Fairy King . . . erm . . .

William Shakespeare   Oberon.

Christopher Marlowe   Oberon. They could be having a tiff and he might – *enchant* the weaver so that he looks hideous . . .

William Shakespeare   We have that ass's head in the props basket!

Christopher Marlowe   Oh Will, Will, you and that damned ass's head. I cannot believe you planned to use that in *Richard III* . . .

William Shakespeare   It would have worked. 'A horse, a horse! My kingdom for a horse . . . oh, *you'll* do!'

Christopher Marlowe   *Anyway* . . . And then Oberon might *enchant* her so that she falls in love with him . . .

Shakespeare *takes out a pen and starts to write on the back of his script . . .*

Christopher Marlowe   Ah, I see you have it already buzzing in your mind, eh?

William Shakespeare   Yes, yes, thank you Kit!

Christopher Marlowe (*he watches him write for a second or two*)   I must go, Will, I'm meeting Ingram Frizer in Deptford . . . my financial worries, you know . . .

William Shakespeare   Oh, Kit. Not Frizer – he is a con man, I hear.

Christopher Marlowe   Will, I am a man more sinned against than sinning . . .

William Shakespeare   Take care, my friend. Call on me tomorrow – we can talk more about this pestilential draft . . .?

Marlowe *leaves.* **Shakespeare** *returns to his tankard and his writing.*

William Shakespeare   Hmm . . . 'more sinned against than sinning . . . '

He makes a note. **Ridcully**, **Rincewind** *and* **Stibbons** *enter, carrying tankards.*

Ridcully   Master Shakespeare? Will? May I call you Will? I am, sir, your greatest fan! Stibbons – get Master Shakespeare another pint of this truly appalling ale, will you?

Stibbons *hands him his own tankard.* **Ridcully** *hands it to* **Shakespeare**. *They all sit at the table.*

Ridcully   Here, sir.

Now – where was I? Oh yes, I really enjoyed that play of yours. Magnificent I thought.

William Shakespeare   Which one was that, good sir?

Lifting the tankard.

Your health.

He goes back to thinking about the plot he and **Marlowe** *discussed.*

Ridcully (*struggling*)   Er – the one with the, er, king in it!

Opposite **Ridcully**, *but unseen by* **Shakespeare**, **Rincewind** *and* **Stibbons** *are trying to mime 'shrew'.*

Ridcully   The rabbit. The rat. The ferret . . .

They point to their ears, then their heads.

Sounds like . . . hat . . .? Rat! I *said* rat!

They mime 'smaller'.

Rodent, thing with teeth – shrew! Shrew!

Stibbons *leans in and whispers.*

Ridcully   Something about a tame shrew . . . A man married to a shrew . . . (*To* **Stibbons**.) Really? A shrewish woman – of course, haha – no one would actually marry a real shrew – haha, ludicrous idea!

Taming of the Shrew. Yes.

William Shakespeare (*becoming aware he was being spoken to . . . vaguely*)   Er . . . thank you.

Ridcully   Now I'm sure you get this all the time . . .

He slaps him on the back.

But we've an idea for you. Too many kings, that's been your problem so far. What the public wants now, what puts bums on seats –

Rincewind   Feet.

Ridcully   What?

Rincewind   Bums on feet, Archchancellor. It's mostly standing room in the theatre he uses.

Ridcully (*dubiously*)   Feet, then. Bums, anyway. Cheers!

They all 'cheers' and drink.

Bums on, haha, feets.

He drinks more.

Funny thing, funny thing – something similar happened to us 'smatteroffact, few years back. Midsummer's Eve – these chaps were goin' to put on a dance, er, *play* for the king; next thing, elves all over the place, haha.

Why thank you, Stibbons, I certainly will have another. This stuff is far too sweet to be a serious drink . . .

Stibbons *exits and returns in a moment or two with two more tankards.*

Ridcully   Where was I? Ah. Elves. What you've got to do, what you've gotta do . . . is . . .

Why aren't you writing all this down?

Rincewind *passes him a modern study guide of* A Midsummer Night's Dream, *which he furtively opens.*

Ridcully   Y'see, Theseus, Duke of . . . *(he checks)* . . . Ay-thens . . . is planning to marry, erm, Hippo-lighter.

Rincewind *whispers.*

Ridcully   Hippolyta? Queen of the A-maze-ons, y'see. And it's around midsummer . . .

Blackout.

Scene Six

An area in Elizabethan London. Timbers creak. This appears to be a rehearsal for A Midsummer Night's Dream, *but it turns out to be the* **Elves** *trying it out. They each carry manuscript copies of their roles.*

Greysteel (Puck)
    The king doth keep his revels here tonight:
    Take heed the queen come not within his sight;
    For Oberon is passing fell and wrath,

Vinculus (Moth)
    Either I mistake your shape and making quite,
    Or else you are that shrewd and knavish sprite
    Call'd Robin Goodfellow: are not you he
    That frights the maidens of the villagery;
    Are not you he?

Greysteel (Puck)
　Thou speak'st aright;
　I am that merry wanderer of the night.
　I jest to Oberon and make him smile
　But, room, fairy! here comes Oberon.

Vinculus (Peaseblossom)
　And here my mistress. Would that he were gone!

Enter, from one side, **Oberon**, *with his train; from the other,*
Titania, *with hers*

Lankin (Oberon)
　Ill met by moonlight, proud Titania.

Elf Queen (Titania)
　What, jealous Oberon! Fairies, skip hence:
　I have forsworn his bed and company.

Lankin (Oberon)
　Tarry, rash wanton: am not I thy lord?

Elf Queen (Titania)
　Then I must be thy lady: but I know
　When thou hast stolen away from fairy land,
　Your buskin'd mistress and your warrior love,
　To Theseus must be wedded, and you come
　To give their bed joy and prosperity.

Lankin (Oberon)
　How canst thou thus for shame, Titania,
　Glance at my credit with Hippolyta,
　Knowing I know thy love to Theseus?

Elf Queen (Titania)
　These are the forgeries of jealousy:
　We are their parents and original.

Lankin (Oberon)
　Do you amend it then; it lies in you:
　Why should Titania cross her Oberon?

I do but beg a little changeling boy,
To be my henchman.

Elf Queen (Titania)
Set your heart at rest:
The fairy land buys not the child of me.
His mother was a votaress of my order:
And for her sake do I rear up her boy,
And for her sake I will not part with him.

Lankin (Oberon)
How long within this wood intend you stay?

Elf Queen (Titania)
Perchance till after Theseus' wedding-day.
If you will patiently dance in our round
And see our moonlight revels, go with us;

Lankin (Oberon)
Give me that boy, and I will go with thee.

Elf Queen (Titania)
Not for thy fairy kingdom. Fairies, away!
We shall chide downright, if I longer stay.

*The **Elf Queen** walks off with **Greysteel** and **Vinculus**.*

Lankin (Oberon)
Well, go thy way: thou shalt not from this grove
Till I torment thee for this injury.

Elf Queen (*re-entering, with the others*)   . . . and those
Discworld humans have been showing a great interest in this
man? This Will-eye-am Shakes-pair . . . ?

The other elves attempt a couple of other pronunciations to help her.

Lankin (*speaking over them*)   Yes, your majesty.

Elf Queen   This . . . play . . . is good. It treats us . . . kindly.
We are firm but fair with mortals. We offer rewards to those
who deal well with us. Our beauty is satisfactorily referred
to. Our . . . issues with our husband are dealt with more

romantically than I would like, but nevertheless it is positive.
It enhances us. It places us even more firmly in the human
world.

She looks at the manuscript.

And one of the Discworlders was carrying these?

Lankin (*hesitantly*)   Our grip is loosening, majesty.
Humanity is becoming more . . . questioning.

Elf Queen (*sharply*)   You think it will do us harm? Is it a plot
against us?

The other **Elves** *exchange glances.*

Vinculus   We think it may be.

Elf Queen   How? In what way?

Greysteel   We know that the Discworlders have been seen
in the company of the author.

Elf Queen   Ah! Then perhaps they are endeavouring to *stop*
him from writing this play . . . have you thought of *that*?

Silence.

Can you see *any way* in which these words harm us?

Lankin   We are agreed that we cannot. Nevertheless, we
have a sense that in some way –

Elf Queen   It's so *simple*! At last we are done some real
honour and the Discworlders will try to stop it!

She waves the script.

This just needs a little refinement to ensure we gain
strength. Are you so stupid that you cannot see *that*?

She storms out. There is an embarrassed silence.

Lankin   Humans are a valuable crop. I concede that.
There's never been a species like them for sheer depth of
awe, terror and superstition. No other species can create

such monsters in their own heads . . . but sometimes, you know, I just wonder if they're really worth the effort . . .

Lankin *starts to exit. The others follow.*

Vinculus (*as they start to exit*)   Purely out of interest . . . can any of *us* put a girdle around the Earth in forty minutes?

Greysteel   That would be a very big girdle.

Vinculus   And would *you* want to be called Peaseblossom?

Lankin   I think not.

They exit. Blackout.

Scene Seven

The Globe Theatre, London. **Shakespeare** *enters to polite applause.*

William Shakespeare   O for a Muse of fire, that would ascend the brightest heaven of invention,

A kingdom for a stage; but pardon, gentles all, and let us, ciphers to this great account,

On your imaginary forces work.

Suppose within the girdle of these walls is now confined most ancient Ay-thens,

Piece out our imperfections with your thoughts;

Think when we talk of forests, that you see them; for the which supply, admit me – Will Shakespeare who, prologue-like, your humble patience pray,

Gently to hear, kindly to judge, my play.

Polite applause. He bows and exits. Fanfare. **Burbage** (*as* **Theseus**) *and* **Kent** (*as* **Hippolyta**) *enter. Another actor enters are Philostrate.*

Richard Burbage (Theseus)   Now, fair Hippolyta, our nuptial hour draws on apace; four happy days bring in another moon: but, O, methinks, how slow this old moon wanes! She lingers my desires, like to a step-dame or a dowager long withering out a young man revenue.

Thomas Kent (Hippolyta)   Four days will quickly steep themselves in night; four nights will quickly dream away the time; and then the moon, like to a silver bow new-bent in heaven, shall behold the night of our solemnities.

The lights cross-fade to **Ridcully**, **Angua** *and* **Stibbons** *in the balcony. The play continues as a recording under the next dialogue.*

Ridcully   This theatre stuff is dam' dull. It'll never catch on – you mark my words. Who was that fellow in the [*whatever colour used*] tights?

Angua   That was Master Shakespeare, Archchancellor. The playwright? He was the Prologue. You have to have him at the beginning so everyone knows what the play's about.

Ridcully   Useless. Still can't understand a word of it. What's a gentle, anyway?

Angua   Type of maggot.

Ridcully   Charming. 'Hallo maggots, welcome to the show.' What's this bit?

Angua   Well, *he* thinks that *he* loves *her*, but in fact he really loves *her* . . .

Ridcully   But 'she' *is* a man. In a straw wig. Makin' his voice squeaky.

Angua   Yes, well, in these days, Archchancellor, women aren't allowed to be actors. All the women are played by men.

Ridcully   Why?

Stibbons   They don't allow women on the stage, sir.

Ridcully   Hmpf. Ridiculous. (*In a loud voice.*) There's a man over on the side there whispering to them!

Angua (*whispering*)   He's a *prompter*. He tells them what to say.

Ridcully   Don't they *know*?

Stibbons   But the play does seem to be going quite well, Archchancellor . . . no sign of any elves at all.

Ridcully   Y'know . . . this chap would write much better plays if he didn't have to have actors in 'em. They seem t'get in the way all the time!

Short pause.

I read that *Comedy of Errors* last night. Could see the 'error' right there. There wasn't any '*comedy*'! Thank gods for snack sellers!

Pause.

No sign of elves y'say? I don't like it. It's too quiet. Rincewind's backstage, right? Keepin' an eye out and tryin' to look inconspicuous?

Stibbons   Er . . . yes. Archchancellor.

*Cross-fade to backstage. Timbers creak. Through upstage curtains, we see the actors, facing the back wall (their audience). It is later in the play. As soon as an actor in a donkey head goes onto the stage, the curtains are 'shut' by **Rincewind**, who is peering onto 'the stage'. Suddenly, the **Elf Queen** enters.*

Elf Queen   Ah, potato man.

Rincewind   Potato man? Now, look, just because I like a . . .

*The **Elf Queen** gestures and **Rincewind** freezes.*

Elf Queen   We know everything, wizard. We have seen your friends out there, but they won't be able to do anything. The show will go on, you know – exactly as written.

Rincewind (*through frozen lips*)   . . . will go on . . .

Elf Queen   We know you told Mr Shakespeare a garbled version. And a lot of nonsense it was. So I appeared to him in his room and put the whole thing into his mind. The elegant and charming Fairy Queen . . . her mischievous but likeable attendants. So simple.

Rincewind (*to himself*)   . . . roast potatoes, boiled potatoes . . .

Elf Queen (*ignoring him*)   Can't you hear the applause? They like us. They actually like us. We'll be in their paintings and stories from now on. You'll never get us out of here . . .

Rincewind   . . . pommes frites . . . sauté . . . duchesse . . .

Elf Queen   Don't you think about anything but potatoes?

Rincewind   . . . butter, melted cheese . . .

Elf Queen and Rincewind (*together, as the* **Elf Queen** *reads* **Rincewind**'s *thoughts*)   . . . chopped chives, rosemary, all we have to do is nothing and we've won . . .

Elf Queen   What?

Rincewind (*aloud, quickly*)   Mash! Huge mounds of mash!

Elf Queen   You're trying to hide something, wizard! What is it?

Rincewind   . . . potato cakes, fried potato skins, potato croquettes – no, not those, no one ever does them right . . .

Elf Queen   So – you think only mysteries last? Knowledge is *un*belief? Seeing is *disbelieving*?

Ha!

The play is not over yet, wizard. But it's going to stop. Right now.

The **Librarian** *emerges behind her and crowns her with an iron pan. Creaking timber stops instantly.*

Rincewind   Ha, madam. I think she's had her chips?

The **Librarian** *lifts the pan again.*

Rincewind   Er . . . 'Fried food – bad for your elf '? . . . All right, all right. Sorry!

Librarian   Ook.

Blackout. In the dark, we hear the sound of a fracas, then applause, cheers, calls of 'author, author' . . .

Scene Eight

Outside the Globe, London. There is applause, off.

Ridcully, Angua, Rincewind, Stibbons *and the* **Librarian** *enter, separately.* **Ridcully, Rincewind** *and* **Stibbons** *look a little dishevelled and are out of breath.*

Ridcully   Best not to wait for a curtain call, I thought.

Stibbons   Did you see me wallop that elf with a horseshoe?

Ridcully   Yes. Pity it was an actor. The *other* one was the elf. Still – not a *complete* waste of a horseshoe.

Angua   But we certainly showed them, right? Did we get the . . . little people back . . .?

Ridcully   The *little* people? What 'little people'?

Stibbons (*with a sigh*)   The Senior Wrangler, Chair of Indefinite Studies, the Bursar . . .?

Ridcully   Oh yes. Of course . . .

The **Librarian** *holds up a cage containing the little figures. He passes it to* **Angua**.

Ridcully (*he waves at the little figures*)   Welcome back, gentlemen!

(*Turns to* **Stibbons**.) *That's* goin' t'be a challenge for the faculty to sort out back home, right?

Stibbons *shrugs.* **Ridcully** *looks at the figures in the cages.*

Ridcully   Ah. So – did we win, Mr Stibbons?

Stibbons (*taking out* **Hex**)   Hex?

Hex   The history is completed. Elves will be viewed as fairies and such they will become. Over the course of several centuries belief in them will dwindle as they are moved into the realms of art and literature. They will become a subject suitable for the amusement of children. Their influence will be severely curtailed but it will never die away completely.

Stibbons   *Never?*

Hex   There will always be some influence. Minds on this world are extremely susceptible.

Ridcully   Yes, but we've pushed imagination to the next stage, right? People can imagine that the things they imagine are imaginary . . .

He pauses and looks at **Stibbons** *who nods that this did make sense.*

Ridcully   Elves are little fairies. Monsters get pushed off the map. You can't fear the unseen when you can see it, yes?

Hex   There will be new kinds of monsters. Humans are very inventive in that respect.

Rincewind   Heads . . . on . . . spikes.

Hex   Many heads.

Ridcully   There's always heads on spikes somewhere. Come on, let's go.

Angua   There're still elves here. They're persistent. Something could still go wrong . . .

Ridcully   I think not, Captain. And Mr Rincewind will be keeping an eye on them. Come *on!*

They all start to exit.

Rincewind (*holding back the* **Librarian**)   Um . . . in one of the alternative pasts, I picked up this book – thought you might like it for the Library . . .?

He hands him 'The Oxford Companion to Edward de Vere, Earl of Oxford'.

It's pretty far-fetched, but I mean, I suppose it *could* have happened? In one of the infinite legs of the trousers of time . . .?

The **Librarian** *takes the book and shrugs.*

*They exit, passing two of the audience (***Queen Elizabeth** *and* **Bess, Countess of Shrewsbury***) as they go. They have programmes for* A Midsummer Night's Dream.

Queen Elizabeth   The bit with the queen and the man with the ass's head was absolutely hilarious, Bess.

Bess, Countess of Shrewsbury   Aye, madam, it was.

Queen Elizabeth   And the wall bit, too. (*She laughs.*) When the man said 'He is no crescent, and his horns are invisible within the circumference' I nearly . . . well, were I not just a weak and feeble woman, I might have widdled my breeches. If I was wearing breeches, of course.

I do like a good laugh, as you know, Bess.

They exchange a look, then both laugh at this one.

Bess, Countess of Shrewsbury   Aye, ma'am. You are known for your wacky sense of humour. Many courtiers have laughed their heads right off!

But I didn't understand why all those people in the [*describes the* **Elves'** *appearance*] and stuff were chased across the stage by the man in the hairy red costume . . .

Queen Elizabeth   Ah – we think he was meant to be Spanish . . . you know how our people think.

Bess, Countess of Shrewsbury   Of course, madam. But why did those men – and that woman in the kilt – get onto the stage too – and why was that man in the red dress running around shouting about potatoes?

Queen Elizabeth   Whatever *they* might be.

Bess, Countess of Shrewsbury   Quite so, madam. And while Puck was speaking at the end I definitely thought I could hear a fight going on.

Small pause.

Queen Elizabeth   Experimental theatre.

Bess, Countess of Shrewsbury   Good dialogue though, madam.

Queen Elizabeth   And all credit to Mr Burbage's actors, the way they kept going regardless.

Bess, Countess of Shrewsbury   Yes, madam. And I could have sworn there was *another* Queen up on stage at one point early in the play. And she looked like a woman! You know- the one who was trying to strangle the potato man.

Queen Elizabeth   A woman? On stage? Don't be ridiculous. We would not countenance such an outrage. Good play, though.

Bess, Countess of Shrewsbury (*as they start to leave*)   And frankly, your majesty, I don't think you could *get* a girdle that big.

Queen Elizabeth (*as they both exit*)   Yes. It would be dreadful if special effects took over from the magic of live theatre.

They exit. Bare stage for a moment. Then a banana drops onto the stage. Fade to blackout.

www.ingramcontent.com/pod-product-compliance
Lightning Source LLC
Chambersburg PA
CBHW060808110426
42739CB00032BA/3143